Life

Hollis Dixon

chipmunkapublishing

the mental health publisher

Published by

Chipmunkapublishing

PO Box 6872

Brentwood

Essex CM13 1ZT

United Kingdom

http://www.chipmunkapublishing.com

Chipmunkapublishing gratefully acknowledge the support of Arts Council England.

Biography

Born in 1969. Youngest of eight children, Hollis Dixon had a normal comprehensive education, leaving school with 3 o' levels and 5 CSEs also unrecognised o'level art which was done in his spare time. He had a good working life from school age up until 2009 in various jobs, mainly the care industry and security reaching management level in warehouse, care and security posts. He was first diagnosed with psychosis at age 24 after 2 years of substance abuse, suffering with visual and audio illusions of which he knows now were not illusions at all, but an awareness of a different plane of life.

He had two main relapses of which the first caused a breakdown of a 9 year relationship with two children and second relapse caused the breakdown of a 3 year relationship with one child at age 32. Both times the same state was reached without any substance abuse at all. He became homeless in 2010 which he sees as an enlightening and spiritual time. His awareness was heightened and his spiritual experiences were a daily occurrence; so much so that it became the norm. He sees art and writing as a positive vent of emotions and oneself and the future, we will see.

Hollis Dixon

I thought I'd found sanctuary. Wood floors, large windows, one exit, one entrance. Amenities accessible in every way. Ten minutes' walk and the skyline from east to west were fields and foliage and the place to be. Until one late evening I sat thinking in the living room focusing on the dark wooden floors which covered the area of the flat and its grain turned into a graveyard of open coffins. Each one with a skeleton with arms crossed and feet like they were pinned together. They covered the floor from corner to corner. Where ever I looked was a skull smiling with its uncovered teeth. Although this image was unnerving, there was a peaceful calm surrounding me and the thought was not to leave, but to stay as I was home. An afterthought about the image of coffins in the living room came to me I remembered a picture seen in a history book of the way slave traffickers used to fill their ships when transporting slaves; they were packed in like sardines at the bottom of the ships laying in the same position as the skeletons. I thought could this vision have been a warning. Also I used to find myself waking up in this position; feet together, arms crossed with my hands on each shoulder. In a rigged state unable to move.

The events that follow from that day changed my view on life and what life is. Life was not as it seemed or as I saw it while growing up within the boundaries of society. Time passed maybe 2 or 3 weeks in a normal existence but with the thought of a graveyard in my living room. One evening, thoughts raced through my mind, why this, why that, as soon as I had reached one conclusion another question would present itself. Efforts to sleep were pointless and to calm my manic thought processes which were drawing the energy from my body. Leaving me in a lethargic state but with a tense overactive mind. I lay awake contemplating all and all one could until sunrise, then a short sleep, maybe thirty minutes or so was ended with a vision which changed everything. I woke up and looked over at my fitted wardrobes and there amongst the clothes was a hand on an outstretched arm with its finger pointing at the bed and myself. I closed my eyes and looked away thinking that it was not really there. I looked again and it was still there with its dark shirt sleeves and ruffled cuff. I stared as it retracted slowly, pulling its finger into a close fist before the arm went backwards into the wardrobe between the pile of t shirts. Was I chosen, or was I blamed? I did not move from my bed for a while. lay there thinking about what just happen. Was I going crazy, or have I entered into the paranormal plane. What have I done to be chosen or blamed. There was a point while I lay there when I got really frightened. Was this what happened when you are going to die or the beginning for real life, and what I was living before was just a childs playground and now I have to grow up and face the real world. Finally got up and got dressed and sat in the living room, still trying to gather my thoughts together and get on with the day. I didn't sleep in that room for 3 days. When I plucked up the courage to enter the room again, I looked for a way of entry from the back of the wardrobe, there was none. As that was one of the main thoughts I was having for the past three days. A solid wall separates the room from a small car park along the high street. Now the normal explanation was no longer a option. Thoughts of what was happening was real, but just not of what I had known before. And I was willing to move forward and know more. Life from then on became a learning experience, whatever I did seemed like it was planned, controlled and protected by something which I now know was nature. The manic thought process always was followed by a strange happening or spiritual experience.

My reading at this time was Carlos Castaneda "Second ring of power" and "journey to ixland" and the philosopher's dictionary "Mind". I read them in turn, depending on what mood I was in. I used to walk to nearby nature reserve and sit looking over the river and read for hours at a time. I call that bench I used to sit at, my spot. There I was as close as I could be to nature and where we all come from. I experienced inspirational thoughts and was communicating with the elements, which seemed to guide me through many a difficult time.

One night while writing on my laptop, I noticed out the corner of my eye, something moving in the bedroom. It was like a shadow of a person. At first I was scared, but that quickly passed and a calm thought of not being alone was a comfort. Night after night, these sightings became more frequent. So much so that I was worried when I didn't see them. They became my companions in my stay in this flat. I used to lay awake in my bed looking into my living room, watching them pass to and fro through my open bedroom door. Although eerie at times, the feeling when they were about was calm and peaceful but yet intense. I used to find things moved around the flat, even missing. I did get a bit paranoid at first, but found that the things that went missing I did not need, and the things that were moved when I really needed them, I found. I became so familiar with the shadows that there were times when I saw them in the same room, seeing them walk in and out at their own will. Also features could be made out like male, female, type of clothing they were wearing. This is when I would see them as an image and not a shadow, which didn't happen very often. In the daylight they would look like a figure of water but solid. One day I was washing up a few glasses in the kitchen and I was in a calm, focused state of mind. I placed a small tumbler upside down on the draining board. I looked away; there was a clink of glasses. I looked back on the draining board and it was the right way up. I thought for a minute that I put it that way and so I replaced it upside down. I carried on washing up and again a clink of glasses and it was the right way up again. I looked at the gap I put the tumbler in and there was not enough room for it to spin 180 degress. So I could not have balanced it on its edge, and it somehow spun the right way up. It had to be picked up turned and placed in same gap. My thoughts were the shadows were letting me know that they were not just spirits but physical and they had no intention to hurt me. This opened my mind to the unknown.

Days after while sitting reading the philosophers dictionary one afternoon I came to notice a movement around me, it was strange because it was not as large as the shadows I normally see. It was like a small figure; no more than a foot and a half high made of water, transparent but yet solid. I could not make out what its shape was. It moved quickly, darting around the room. It seemed to be able to move through walls and solid matter. It would dart into the kitchen , then appear in the hall. I watched it for a good while trying to work out what it reminded me of. I was comfortable with its presence and as time went on, I noticed it was with me in the car, when I went out for walks, even when I had company. Also the human- like figures began to show themselves in the same manner. Water like during the day and like shadows at night but solid in both cases. More and more this happened and I became accustomed to them being around day and night. After a pleasant evening without much activity with the figures, I went to bed and was awoken by an intense feeling like pressure within my head. I was drawn to stand and look out of the living room window. There was a small car parked directly outside the flat I was in, there I saw shadows moving freely amongst the cars; their movements were quick and precise as they emerged from the small alley at the side of the flat. I watched them for a good hour; There were times when it would look like it noticed me watching them, and look at me, and a very short feeling of fright would come over me, but I could not stop watching them. Although eerie, with the feeling that such things live amongst us, I was comforted that they chose me to show themselves to. I went to bed calm and slept well.

During these times the non-verbal communication between myself and the figures grew through thought and feeling. I used to find myself having conversations when they were around where answers to my questions were answered in such a way that I know that the thoughts I was having, were not my own. Concepts and reasoning which I couldn't see how with what I knew I could come to. Conclusions, which as I saw it, were beyond me. Answers, which took many nights of contemplation to make sense of them. One of the things that was said to me through thought was "no negative, no positive, just truth.... This I will carry with me till I die as it answers many questions within that statement. Although very hard to live by this statement, because lots of people can t take the truth and get upset, because of religion, personal views and beliefs, aims and wants. Me included, I try.

It seemed that they were getting more and more comfortable with me and I with them... at times touching me, blowing in my face, lying next to me in bed. The knowledge and perception that I was gaining was hard to understand but the books I had read helped. I would go for long walks in fens nearby and communicate with them learning nature's way. Animals within the fens seemed to react to me in ways that I have not come across before, my state of mind would play a major factor in the way this happened. I have two examples of this; fear, anxiousness in me would make animals warn and protect... when I was calm within myself, they would let me walk among them; horses, cattle, deer, even some birds would come close as if they were tame. I was close to nature, making me think that the figures were part of nature too.

Travelling back from a visit to my parents which was about an hour away, that intense feeling came over me. It was about 12.30am or thereabouts, I was on the main drag into the village I lived in and I was drawn to stop in a layby about a mile outside the village. I sat there for about 15 minutes, looking into the surrounding woodland and the sky above it. There was a large tree that stood on its own at the corner of the forest and next to it was a field. Looking in the night sky I noticed a white owl flying, it seemed like it was circling my car, which it was. It would fly around about 10 or 15 metres from the car and then head back over to the field. This was done many times, too many to count. Then as silently as he came; he disappeared. I went back, looking at the tree which for some reason I was drawn to do so. I stared and focused on it and it seemed to change shape. I looked away, then looked back again and it was like a large figure silhouette crouching down on top of a hill. As I focused, I noticed that one area of the tree was moving in a manner like hand gestures when someone is explaining something. This went on for some time. I sat there for a good hour and a half focusing on the tree, unable to switch my engine back on due to something stopping me. Looking in the direction of the village I saw many lights shooting across the sky. It was like watching an old wartime dog fight with modern planes. And I saw what I can only describe as machine gun fire coming from the large lights. Between the tree and the lights overhead, it kept me distracted for another hour or so, then suddenly I felt the urge to move and head home. I did so in a rush, but as I accelerated away, I looked through the passenger side window and there was the owl no more than 2 metres away, flying alongside the car. A good 5 or so seconds with it in my view before it peeled off and went into the field.

A few days later, I had a normal day in the flat with the mundane everyday things taking up most of the day, apart from a good weight training session in the morning. Filling my evening with Facebook and the T.V., also a glass of wine as I sat in front of my marine fish tank and listening to the goings on within the village from my open window. I went to bed early that night, no tension, stress or strange sightings, but there was a calm about this day, nothing to upset or ruffle my feathers at all. I lay in bed as the evening drew in thinking about nothing much. I noticed that I couldn't feel my head against the pillow, it was like it was floating. That sensation slowly crept its way down my body until I felt nothing, I could only imagine that it felt like being paralysed. It wasn't like weightlessness or flying, just no feeling at all of my hands, feet, leg, chest; I could not feel the bed against me, or the quilt on my chest. I had to calm myself for a moment, I relaxed and just thought, but that was the thing, that all I could do was think and be. A peaceful, lovely feeling I had never felt clarity like that before. I couldn't hear anything, couldn't smell anything, it was like I was just my soul without a body. My senses came back after a while and I was as normal, but it did worry me a bit, so I told a friend, so if it did happen again and I didn't recover then at least someone knew what could have happened to me!

The strange experiences continued. Another night alone after an uneventful day, while lying in bed. I heard a sound like a cat cub playing; a soft playful sound, not angry at all. I attempted to look and see where the sound was coming from and what it was, but something was stopping me, I lay there thinking what it might be. My body became rigid and I couldn't move. This feeling I had had before, so I didn't panic. Just relaxed and waited for it to pass. A few minutes later I felt something on the left side of the bed which lay on my arm. The feeling of it was like it was covered in stiff short hair and about two foot long. I didn't see anything, but that spikey sensation up my arm and a feeling of some weight to it lasted until I fell asleep. After that night the cub like sound was heard in many times and places and it laying next me became a regular occurrence.   Putting two and two together, I realised that the small, water like figure was the same thing that I felt with me from time to time on my arm.   One afternoon, it was mid-summer, sun was shining, people were out in their droves; I was in, for some reason and couldn't leave the flat. Every time I thought of a walk or just popping over to the shop, something would stop me physically; not by a hand on the shoulder or grabbing my arm... I just couldn't put my hand on the door handle. After all that was happening to me over the past few months, I accepted this quickly and sat down in my recliner and began to read. I read all day until I fell asleep in the chair in the evening. I was awoken by that intense but yet calm feeling and pressure in my head.   I opened my eyes slightly, and there, clear as day, three figures came through my unopened door. They all seemed to peer over at me from the hallway. One came over to me and stood with its face next to my ear. One went in the kitchen and the other bedroom. It was like they were searching the place. After about two minutes in which I was still in the chair with one next to me, the other two came out of the rooms and stood by the front door. The one next to me nodded and waved its finger at me as if it was telling me off or something. I took that action as don't say a word. They all met at the door and left. The intensity became calm as they left. No fear, no anxiety, just peace. My companions were getting close to me.

Problems with my car yet again, I see myself as a bit of a boy racer but without the cash. I do all the work on my car myself, well as much as possible; I have tuned, it cleaned it, leathered it, made it look nice, it has a very distinctive sounding exhaust; unique in fact; I know this because I made it myself; all legal but just gives the car a little more go. The problem this time was a front headlight that the lens had broken; straightforward job, so I took the broken headlight off my car that morning and brought it inside where I had the new lens waiting. The job was simple; cut old seal on broken lens, put new lens on and reseal, so I got my Stanley knife and did what I just said. I placed my Stanley knife on the side, in my living room and took the headlight out and fitted it to my car. On my return I went to lock the front door as I normally do but something was stopping me, it was getting dark and the high street was getting a bit lively with all the pub – goers as well as being a small 4 car car - park out the front of my house, it was a main short cut to the local supermarket. I normally lock the door because of the human traffic that passes of a night time. For some reason I stood by my side cabinet where I placed my Stanley knife, and put my hands behind me and leant on them. I stood there focusing on the fact that I couldn't lock my front door; then I noticed that I couldn't move; my hands wedged behind my back. I thought of what could emerge from the situation. Someone may come in and god knows what could happen with me not being able to move. I was worried for a bit, but as time passed and nothing happened, I relaxed a little. I tried to move several times during that hour and a half or so to no avail. Why couldn't I move? I had no idea. Shortly after I managed to slide 1 of my hands out from behind my back and the rest of my body started to co-operate with me. I attempted to lock the front door again but still couldn't. I fixed myself something to eat and sat in front of my fish tank watching the fishes and this relaxed me. I was wondering if I would be able to sleep with door open or not. Went to bed rather late that night, due to the situation I was placed in.

The next morning I was woken up by the butchers who use the car park in front of my flat to load their deliveries. Their loud banter and laughing was pretty annoying at 7.30 in the morning. One of those things you don't know until you move into a new place. I got up to start the day. My front door was still unlocked from the night before. I was relieved that all was ok in the flat and no one came in to my knowledge. My thoughts were; shower, breakfast, then out for a ride or something. This didn't happen; as I went to shower, I felt myself reluctant to do it, I went into the kitchen and opened the fridge and my mind just went blank so I shut it again. My brain was just not functioning. I stood around in the living room for a bit, trying to sort my head out but I ended up going back to bed. I was woken up by the lunchtime washing of vans and cleaning up. I got up in a daze, not knowing what to do with myself... I tried acting as if all was ok, with a shower and getting on with the day, but everything I planned to do was stopped by something; I could not dwell on any thing for more than a second or two, so couldn't get anything done, even down to opening the curtains. I found myself walking around the shady flat, spending silent moments in each room not doing anything constructive at all. This went on well into the evening. The only contact I had with the outside world was being aware of the chat of a couple as they walked through the car park and the odd noise from the neighbours. I went to bed after not eating anything, just drinking water, thinking it would be different tomorrow.

That night I slept well for the first part, all was quiet in the village and human traffic passing my window was minimal. About 4 in the morning, I woke up; my eyes opened into a dark room. I tried to move and couldn't, but this time it wasn't pleasant. My arms were pressed against my chest, my legs felt like they were pinned to the bed and my head forced against the pillow. I panicked and struggled to gain control of my body. I opened my mouth to let out a yell, but nothing came out, but yet I could hear my scream in my head. I tried to kick my legs and lift my arms, it was a hard struggle to move, more than a centimetre. I became out of breath as the struggling tired me, then I relaxed to calm my thoughts and work out what was going on and just then I was released out of whatever was holding me to my bed. I got up and went and sat in the living room for a while thinking this has happened before when I was on holiday in Jamaica and I should have controlled myself and not panicked. It was a frightening experience as my eyes were open and I could see that there was no logical reason to be pinned down like that. I sorted my head out and went back to bed hoping that it would not happen again.

That morning I was woken up by a van driving into the car park at the usual time; 7.30. the butchers were very quiet that morning for some reason. They got on with whatever they were doing without many words exchanged. This gave me a little peace for a lie in. I got up mid morning, was in a thoughtful mood, still in a bit of a state due to the last nights happenings. My actions and what I did were slow and well thought out, even down to opening the fridge I would try and think of all the outcomes of each of my actions. This made everything take a long time. I had a bath and by this time, it must have been 12.30 as the butchers were back in the yard. I was thinking of going out. One of the delivery men was on the phone outside my window talking loudly. My curtains were drawn as I was unable to open them for some reason, so I just listened as he walked up and down passed the window. I tried just to get on with what I was doing, but noticed that his words were having an effect on my actions. I couldn't focus on what I wanted to do because of his loud voice distracting my thoughts, so much so that I was stopped in my tracks as he talked. So I just stood in my living room until he finished. This worried me a bit; was the fact that I couldn't lock my door or open my curtains because of people's words and actions outside? I became focused on the situation which might come out of this if that sort of control was possible. And why it was happening to me. Another day without leaving the flat, a lot of thinking and a little reading took up most of the time that day. I was managing to eat, which was a good thing, but food was slowly running out as I was unable to go to the store to buy more. The activity with the shadows was still on-going, seeing them most days and nights; that was just the norm for me now. It was a great comfort that they were there. The manic thoughts of the situation were some how justified by the thoughts that I exchanged with them. But in doing so was going ever deeper into an understanding of life which was not the norm. It seem like my thoughts were being controlled so my body followed.

In the evening as I was watching T.V, I heard my car start; the exhaust sound was un-mistakable, the car was parked just at the end of the small alley to the left of my flat in the supermarket car-park. I turned the T.V down and listened as it stood there ticking over, I tried to get up to go and have a look, but yet again I couldn't seem to control myself to get out of the door. I stood there saying to myself; is it, or isn't it my car? I still had the only keys for it. The car was running for about ten minutes in which I became in a panic state, trying to bring myself to leave the flat...What ever that was controlling me was not a physical one, but it was controlling my mind. Making me doubt myself and making my action hard or impossible. My mind was racing about what was happening to the car I loved so much. Then I heard it reverse and wheel spin off. I forced myself up and went to the front door; just then my mind went blank and was unable to but my hand on the handle. Frustration set in as I kept trying to leave the flat... My frustration became anger and I began to stomp around approaching the front door not actually being able to grab hold of the handle to open it. Why is this happening? What would I do without my car? Who has taken it? I even thought of phoning the police, but how could I when I had not even been outside to check if it was there or not? I eventually calmed down, but was in a trance like state, just focusing on the floor trying to work out what I could do to combat this mind control. About thirty minutes later, I heard it again; the engine racing and wheels spinning in the car park. My mood changed instantly; frustration and anger and serious tension. Time passed and I had to accept that I couldn't leave the flat; and I couldn't do much about the car. I relaxed by watching the marine fish swim effortlessly in my tank, but still questioning what was happening to me. Curtains drawn with just the light from my tank, I sat and thought of all conclusions that may occur from my car being taken – good and bad. The fact that getting a job would be harder as the nearest mind town was 30 minutes away. Visiting family couldn't happen easily . The trips to sign on would a long bus ride to next town. And I had just lost my hobby and past time. It was very late when I went to bed anticipating the driver which wakes me up at 7.30.

7.30 came around quickly, the sound of the van pulling up in front of my window woke me up... another day, I thought to myself. As usual the voices from outside were loud and annoying. I could feel the sound in the pit of my stomach as the words rang out. I lay in bed listening as there wasn't much else I could do. I noticed from time to time what they were talking about could have been related to me... Were they the reason I was stuck inside like a prisoner? Paranoid you might think; but some things that were said were so close to the truth of what I was experiencing, it was uncanny. I tried to look through the curtains to see which one was talking about me, but yet again I was unable to move the curtains. I just had to sit and listen to the different tones in their voices, hoping that when I could get out I will be able to remember and put a voice to a face. This was a serious wind up; the mornings always used to put in me in a thoughtful, focused state, of which I mean; lots of thinking but not much doing. I got up about 9am after the drivers had left for their deliveries. I thought I must check on my car and got dressed and had something to eat. At that time, my state of mind was not a good one; annoyed about what the drivers were saying; annoyed about what happened to my car, annoyed about not being able to leave my flat, but I comforted myself with my thoughts of saying that it was just meant to be but also thought that I was being controlled by something that doesn't value the normal way of life; eating, sleeping, shopping, my contact with others meant nothing. The thoughts I was having were stretching my understanding of life to its limits, but in saying that there seemed to be no limit to the possibilities of my new understanding.

My frustrations grew worse, constant tension in my head with questions. My awareness was at a point where I would notice things before they happened, like I could feel people; as people walked through the car park, I get a feeling in my stomach before they would reach my window and see their shadow go past and my mood would change like I was feeling theirs. I was relying on senses that I didn't know I had.

At lunchtime, I sat in my recliner, trying to read, which was difficult and the thought that the driver is coming entered my head; with that thought, a feeling in my chest which was uncomfortable, not more than a second or 2 after; up drove the van. This made me go into a frenzy of thought; what if the mood I was in was caused by the people around me? Are my thoughts governed by moods and thoughts and moods of others? Is this what my companions were teaching me? To realise my natural senses to live? Were the people outside talking and acting in such a way on purpose to control me like this? Will this end? I began to pace from my bedroom to the living room and back again, up and down, up and down; as I paced I had my head down and eyes focused hard on the floor and each step I took. This went on for hours, I must have done a good few miles. Thoughts on the conclusions raced through my mind , frustrating me even more, I got angry many times but managed to control it until something clicked in me, maybe a voice from outside or a thought in my head made me shout; "do I have to get upset every day?" As I looked up through the curtain window; that seemed to do the trick; I felt instant calm. I sat down to rest. It wasn't long before the thought process started again, this time thinking is this a test to push me to my limit, or over the edge; or was the mental energy that this situation was creating in me helping or hindering those around me, because if I can feel them; they must be able to feel me. Food was running out, and my fish were out of bloodworm. No-one had contacted me for days, maybe this was it; me from now on! I slowly accepted that as a fact and started believing without a doubt all my feelings and thoughts, enjoying the fact that I could feel people and what they were thinking and that each feeling reflected the mood or intention of the people outside. It seemed like the more I was put in situations where there was a build up of stress or tension, the more energy would build up within me and I became more sensitive to the people and my surroundings. I could tell when a person was about to enter the car park, not all the time but most, I sensed when the drivers were going to arrive before they did; voices outside became feelings as well, some pleasant, others not. Approaching people would wake me up out of naps I used to have during the day. Just by feeling them and not by the noise they made. I had time to analyse all that was happening around me, tying them up to my actions and feelings and thoughts within the flat. This went on for a further 3 days, taking a mental note of all I could to back up the fact that thought and feeling can be transmitted and received from person to person. The banter from the butchers in the morning usually started a tension process, gradually gaining momentum during the day as more happened outside and around me. Most nights the tension put me in a trance like state of pure focus making the communication between me and my companions easy and fruitful in answers and realisation about my life and life in general. I began to act according to the way I was thinking and not as I knew before these days of solitary started.. It was all calm and peaceful but with an undercurrent of tension to keep me focused and on the right level of thought. I found myself staring into the sky from my kitchen window which overlooked a secluded garden with high fences. Not looking at anything in particular but somehow gaining information to help me cope with the situation I was in. the thoughts I would have were enlightening and profound. They kept me calm and together. On that 3rd evening I sat down and tried to put down on paper what it was like to be in the situation and the awareness I was living in. I wrote:

Few days in solitary

Although i have not been here, this title is just a feeling... I could call this the beginning of the end, but it would not be timed right as the beginning started without me knowing....

Take most of my writing in consideration, a few days in side closed doors, with only thoughts and stimulants from outside curtained windows and prompts which i mention before. You can't help and I mean can't help but enter into whatever is put into or in front of you...

A reality with feeling... vision... substance. Which you cannot deny but only question...

I have said once that believing is seeing, not seeing is believing... A few days in this situation can confirm this not only seeing but feeling and living...

Also within this time, buildup of feelings of frustration, which breeds anger, reasoning and clarity, causes moments of unexplained vents of energy which make perfect sense within the frame of mind that the situation creates? But to the reality of most of the world, be sectionable I think... But that's only due to what is known as the norm...

Mysteries of the mind, don't underestimate them. You'd be a fool to!

That night I went to bed at about 12.30, very tired and aware of the state of mind I was living in. I fell asleep very quickly, but after a while I woke up and it was still dark with the moon shining in through the thin curtains. I was lying on my back with the quilt just about covering my belly button. I looked to my right at my bedside table and my shoulder and arm caught my eye; it was black, like I had a sweater on. I looked at my chest and it was a completely different colour. I didn't move, I just stared at my arm, it looked like I was looking at an arm of a shadow. I didn't panic, I watched as my arm re-gained its colour like someone putting pieces of a jigsaw together. As each piece went into place, my natural colour came back. It took about ten seconds; piece by piece, my arm and shoulder gained its colour again. I thought that I caught the tail end of my body changing from what I can only say was a shadow. I slept soon after with no distress at all.

Next morning I woke up just as the first driver was turning into the car park. It looked like they were on form with the banter. As usual loud laughter and friendly fire went on between them from 7.30 till about 9. It went quiet then, but I was in a tense focused state by that time. Then out of the blue, a new voice joined the crowd and said; "lets open him up and see what we've got". With those words came that feeling within me and it felt like it was directed at me or about me. I got worried; were they stressing me on purpose to think this way? Then reading my thoughts as I read theirs. I sat in the living room waiting for something to happen; nothing did! All the time I grew more and more tense, thinking that this was planned by someone. Then I got the urge to get up and walk to the window. I reached out and opened the curtain slightly. Just then, a man about 6 foot 6 was as wide as he was tall, if you know what I mean ; a body builder or something, walked out of next door. He walked like he'd just learned how to; head down, focused on the floor, he looked very awkward. I thought then that he acted and walked as I felt. He stomped through the car park and turned the corner. I closed the curtain again and sat down. I racked my brain on what had just happened and settled with the conclusion that he was feeling the tension that I was feeling and he had to leave. I went back to bed about 12.30 after the delivery drivers had gone home, I was completely drained.

After a few hours sleep, I got up, had something to eat which was not much, just a tin of fish. I spent the rest of the day relaxing in my recliner, listening to the goings on outside. Went to bed at a reasonable time, unable to sleep, I sat up, awake wondering about the day's events. There was a full length mirror opposite my bed which for some reason I just focused on my reflection. As I did this, I felt my arms go all tingly up to my shoulders and they felt like they were pressed gently against the pillows on each side. I wasn't worried, I just relaxed and went with it. As I stared into the mirror at myself, I noticed that all I could see was up to my shoulders and could see the wall behind me where my head should have been. I kept on blinking and squinting, thinking that it was just the fact that it was dark that I couldn't see my head, but it just wasn't there.   It was a short time maybe ten minutes or so before my head re-appeared; my arms were still in the position beside me with the same sensation of being gently held to the pillows. The tension in the flat grew and I was getting to the point where I was in a trance-like state. I stared into the living room and there was a lot of movement, shadows moving in and out. I watched them for a while and began to see little beads of coloured lights shooting around the room.   The more the lights moved, and the quicker they got, the tenser I became until a figure of a woman, about 6 foot tall, wearing a long jumper, maybe cream or beige, thin faced with a curly bob stood in the hallway looking at me. She was there for about ten seconds before it looked like she mouthed the word no in the drawn out sense, then it was like she was sucked out of the front door. Instant calm; all movement stopped, tension was gone and my arms were released. I lay down drained and fell asleep.

The next morning, I woke up highly charged with energy.   That morning's banter between the butchers was not as normal, but was more pleasant in some way. As I lay in bed, I got into my head that I should go out. The place I had in mind was in the next village about 6 miles away. The weather was hot but windy. The idea was to ride my bike and to get some exercise. I got up, washed and got dressed; combats and a string vest, got my bike ready, checking tyres, gears and that I had all the necessary equipment to fix a blown tyre if I needed to. Surprisingly, I made it out the front door.   I made my way into the high street and stopped at the corner by the butchers shop. They were all out there, it was like they were waiting for me to set off. One turned and smiled and said hello as I rode off. I rode through the main part of the village into the outskirts where horses were tethered to the side of the roads. Then across the main road onto an area which was flat, you could see for miles but also the wind was at its strongest as there were no wind – breaks. I struggled on that part of the journey, but didn't stop. Just before I got into the neighbouring village, I got into an area of the road where it was wide enough to turn a car. There I saw tyre marks like someone was doing burn – outs and doughnuts in a car. With all the thoughts of my car driving off of an evening I immediately put 2 and 2 together. I didn't dwell on it, I just rode on to my destination. When I got there it was about 5 minutes walk along a thin path to get to the river. I walked, taking in all the sights and sounds of nature. A pigeon was a glorious thing to see, the rustling of the rodents in the grass and the odd bird of prey hunted in the fields, gliding effortlessly, even the little flies itching my face were welcomed. All this was a relief to me and total contrast to my days of solitary. I walked to a bench made out of a trunk of a tree, propped my bike up on its stand, lay on the bench and closed my eyes and just listened and felt what was around me. I was there for about an hour with my eyes closed, I heard a rustling just above my head. I tried to open my eyes, but they wouldn't open. I felt a presence standing at the end of the bench, it felt non – threatening, just a strong feeling that I wasn't alone. It wasn't there for long, but while there, I couldn't think of anything for long. My mind just flittered and couldn't hold on to any thoughts for more than a split second. It was like I was re-charging my batteries. The presence left, I got up soon after, ready to face the world again as well as the 6 mile ride home. The ride home was effortless as the wind was behind me. When I got back to the flat, I checked my car. The tyres I bought 3 months ago were worn down to the wire. I thought this was real.

I could go on explaining different experiences that happened to me while in the flat, but I'll leave you with one more... it was evening, mid-week and the pub nearby was very lively that day. I settled down to sleep, but couldn't. I lay there in a darkened room with that intense yet calm feeling in me. While I lay there I noticed my companions moving around the living room, but somehow the whole thing seemed quite different from before. More intense, but it was the movement and shouting of the locals outside seemed to be causing the intense feeling. I wondered if something had happened at the pub or if I had caused some kind of upset. This went on well into the night as I lay there awake. The intensity grew and grew. My companions were moving freely within the flat, but there were more of them than usual. It seemed that it all came to a head and my feelings were at a great height. It was as if something got between myself and the outside a dampening of sound of the outside. All became calm but the activity within the flat grew then a female voice said "don't worry about them out there" it came from my bedroom door. Instant peace came over me. I listened for a while to my companions mumble amongst themselves in my living room, I felt like I was accepted; into what, I don't know, but it felt nice and calm and peaceful. That night I don't deny was a life changing experience for me.

Up until this present day, I still have these sightings and feelings every day. I've been living in different locations and different towns and the experiences continue to happen. The feeling of being stopped and prevented from doing things happens from time to time and I must say, up until now has not put me or others in a dangerous situation, and also, I have been homeless for about three months and was living in my car. Time spent in that situation was the most active when it came to my companions. A few times in the car I have had a shadow sitting in the passenger seat. The small water – like figure that I saw in that flat; cat like, a little smaller than a lynx. I know this because the silhouette was next to me in my car appeared one day after the cub like sound was heard frequently that day.

There is more to life than most can see. It is not sinister, evil or bad; just another plane in which others exist. The next time you see something out the corner of your eye and you say to yourself "it couldn't be", it could!

All these happenings got me thinking, especially about the type of communication that me and the companions had; the communication by thought and feeling and the ability to send and receive thoughts by focusing or eye contact. You must have heard people say that they could feel someone looking at them; what if the feelings they were getting were the thoughts of the other person and because it was alien to their own thoughts, then it could make an unpleasant feeling within them, hence they could feel the stare. I have had experiences that suggest that thoughts can be transmitted through eye contact. One afternoon while working for a care agency as a carer for a couple with 3 children, I had an encounter with a Rottweiler which up to this day I think was a silly move on my part. I used to work late afternoons, so I turned up at the house just before tea time, about 4.30, I walked up the path and as usual I opened the gate to the back yard and there walking around freely was a fully grown Rottweiler of which I had never seen before. Our eyes met through their open gate. It was like they locked together as we looked at each other. My first reaction was tense, but as we stared became calm. I was like in a trance which allowed me to read its thoughts, believe me that I am the first person to get wary of a dog off its lead in a park much less a thirteen stone Rottweiler in a back yard. Its thoughts were pleasant and it had no intention to attack me. Well that was the feeling I got from the eye contact I had with it. I pushed open the gate fully, walked in calmly, went to the back door and knocked. The family let me in and they all were shocked. The owner of the dog who was a cousin of the wife ask how did you get in and in said I just opened the gate and walked in. He himself said he would not have done that knowing what a Rottweiler is like. To this day I believe that there was communication between me and that dog that put us both at ease and allowed me to get on with what I was doing.

Another situation which suggests that information can be passed through eye contact is; I was with my girlfriend and her parents one afternoon in Cambridgeshire, we were all in one room. I was sitting at the table and my girlfriend was making a cup of tea, her parents were talking to each other on the other side of the kitchen diner. My girlfriend came over to me and looked me straight in the eye as she put a cup of tea in front of me. I sensed tension and the thought "Meet me in the garden" came to me... I didn't act on it, but they were the next words my girlfriend said, which I did, because there was something she wanted to say without her parents hearing. In both cases, there was an initial feeling of tension or a slight unpleasant feeling. The eye contact was eye to eye, meaning that my left eye was focused at their right and my right was focused on their left, which is a hard thing to do try it and see. Normally, one eye can only focus on one eye at a time. This leads me to believe that conversation with another or contact with an animal where eye contact is as such, there is more information passed between 2 than just the words and body language which I think pays a big part in everyday life. Do you ever feel uncomfortable or overly happy after a conversation with someone when the words that were exchanged do not warrant the feeling you're having?   Or the words that have been exchanged are not satisfying to you until the person looks at you? These things happen to me a lot.   Spectrums of feelings; happy, sad, tearful, anxious, tense when nothing in my life warrants that feeling.   What I'm saying is that pleasant and unpleasant feelings can be passed between any animal and human not only by eye contact but by one being in a certain awareness' to pick up on others feelings. This could be familiarity of the other person, or just nature's way to make us aware if others instinct.

By looking at this theory wider, if a person or animal was looking and focusing in one direction and in that direction was a person with the awareness to pick up on others thoughts and feelings then eye contact, even sight of the other person is not needed to make the recipient feel what the other is transmitting. My example of this is many times in my life I have felt angry, happy, and anxious when in a room and another has entered the house even without me knowing, causing me to change moods. Moods which reflect the other person's feelings or intentions at that time.   If the person has an unpleasant or bad intention, I was normally drawn to go to that room or situation to calm or diffuse the said situation. Other times that person had come intending to see me or has been thinking about me in a worrying way. I have been drawn to situations where my presence was needed without me knowing that there was a situation at all. I believe that the connection between family, close friends and persons with this kind of awareness accounts for most of the movements of people today. In that I mean, when a person leaves their home going to the shop, the cinema, the pub; whatever the destination, subconsciously without them knowing, they are not only going for a drink, a meal or a film, but to be there to say or do something for someone else's benefit. How many times have you had a problem or issue which you couldn't resolve and you hear someone in a conversation that helps or you meet someone that helps without you arranging it? Also it could be that an action gives you inspiration to come to a conclusion to resolve the issue. I don't believe that there are coincidences, just planned actions governed by feeling and thought by everyone. But in saying that it can also work in an unpleasant way, meaning you could be drawn into a situation which causes an issue or problem like; walking into a pub and seeing your partner with someone else, parking your car somewhere and its clamped or going to the shop and forgetting to pick up your credit card off the counter. The fact that these things happen could be caused by someone else's thought that they are transmitting to you. Far-fetched you might say, but I see telepathy as a fact and can transmit pleasant and unpleasant feelings and thoughts. If your thoughts can be controlled then you can be controlled.... Controlled by the stronger or more aware person who is in tune with themselves and nature. I think that every living thing communicates with each other though eye contact, action, focus and thought. This is done subconsciously without us being aware. Also with the spirit world with thought and feeling. When I say spirit world I don't mean ghost or the dead, but living beings that exist on another plain.

Governor , Governess

I walk and I am not master of myself.. Action reactions are of something that is bigger than man.. The sky tells a story the wind a song.. The creatures of the earth are but signs that guild you on. The peace the oneness with what once was me.. Is me again..
LIFE

The spoken word

Just a thought, the spoken word whether English or other…

The word is a stimulant. Which promotes good or bad or indifferent feelings and emotion within the human body, happiness, sadness, anger, love. These emotions can cause reactions which are not right if you apply this theory. So thought and communication as we know it, is something which as I see it, hinders the progress of life. This is because the word explains, and as far as I know, no one knows the meaning of life. So Then any explanation through the spoken word is just confusing the issue.

Live and love life…

The Hay Stack

Sitting in a field, drinking a nice claret. I ask myself where I go from here. Home you might say. Where is it, home I mean.

I feel more comfortable out here, I smile when there is nothing to smile about, my mind is much clearer out here. I feel like me. So which one is home. What would you say? Home should have all those things. But it doesn't. Does that make this home..?

The green fields, the sun, the sounds which even when loud and alarming are still having a sense of comfort in them.

This hay stack which I visit from time to time somehow is more comfortable than the sofa. To me I can't seem to get my head round where am I supposed to be, or is it just a case of transporting mentally between the two. Transition is difficult at best of times.

The bottle has run out of its contents, and the pedal home is going to be tricky. But it is worth it. A short time out here is a life time really.

Untilthen...........................

Reasons

This has been going on for a while, serious surge of negative thought runs through my mind when you and some others are in the situation with me.

What do you think that might, be.

THE0RIES: Fear as you and others know me so well, can be seen as threat.

Anxiety builds up due to the situation. Triggering negative thoughts therefore, natural defences are put up.

Misunderstanding of the situation, and due to this only can think of negative conclusion or reason.

My way of dealing with situations with certain people.

Or thinking out of the box, the vibes from certain people are negative towards me.

Again out of the box. My interpretation of the vibe is negative.

If these or any of your ideas of which I would prefer yours, make sense please say. Because frankly its pissing me off.

Night shift

Today was a strange day....can't sleep...have not slept at all really...

Good day saying that but still not the norm as late...funny time night. Peacefully yet eerily...just sounds of bubbles from tanks breaking silence..

Mind wonders on this and that. Causes fear, reassurance, comfort and indifferent emotions...

Town not yet alive but I know there is life out here... alone but yet

The TV screen is but distraction from the eerie calm that surrounds you...

Sights of movement and audio sounds, which keeps you alert and awake...

Question is why I am awake....

MONEY

As I look back on things and situations with people when it comes to money I am confused or misled in my thinking.

I see that most people will rather give you time, information or even himself than give you money whether or not they are getting it back.

Now looking at it from a religious point of view, it said in the Bible that the love of money is the route of all evil. This is true in most cases, so saying that it means that the majority of acts in the world are evil. Motivation for most action is money.

I think time, thoughts and ideas from one's self is more important than money. Although money is important, and aid life in a big way, it is man made after all, and what man makes, has a limited life span.

There is not much that money can get you which you take with you all of the time in everyday life. So why do people put so much effort in keeping it. Relationships break down, people are killed, and people are left to suffer. If there's one thing which I can say I cannot comprehend is why the value of money is more than life itself.

So why don't I

One theory I have is that most people are willing to give as long as they are part of the outcome. Boyfriend giving money to a girl for a night out is ok if the boyfriend has some part in the night. This theory can be put to almost all situations where money has been exchange. Parents, friends, partners have the same criteria when it comes to money. But the types of relationships I mention are all supposed to be caring relationships. If they care, then why be selfish.

To a certain extent everyone has to be, if for nothing else, for self - survival.

Block on life

This may explain a lot of things that happen in my life. I would have a thoughtful moment trying to make plans and head towards my aims. I think of what I would do in any given situation, and my mind will switch and think of what another person would do, be it a friend, a loved one or work colleague. This after time has a very bad effect on who I am and my general life situation. I am seen to be someone else. As my actions are not mine. This in turn makes me as a person non- existent to others because what they see is not me. This fits in with my peace about   the myth of free will," the prompts that hamper my thoughts guiding me to think of others, makes me suppress me myself. But in saying that it is not only my mind, which is hampering me, also it is action by others seems to do it too. Physical interference seems to take affect when others are involved. Things go missing; being in the wrong place at the right time is the norm. All are mostly detrimental to myself. Why is the question, and you know what, it doesn't matter. It seems to happen anyway. Love life and learn or try to at least.

HEALTHY BANK OR MENTAL HEALTH

Just a thought,
It seems that people will restrict their life when it comes to money, and look after their bank balance at all costs.

But at the same time risk their mental health in nearly every situation in relationships and contact with people
A person is in financial problems at a stage in his or her life. Advice given to this person is next time to count the pennies, do not borrow, live within your means. All these are to protect that healthy bank balance.

A person has two or three bad relationships, either as friends, partner or even family.
Advice given to this person is get back on the band-wagon, there is Mr. or Mrs. Right out there so keep looking, go and play the field. Just enjoy yourself. Don't give up it will happen.

Money is a physical thing, you can hold it. You can put it away. It has no mind of its own so poses no threat to you as a person at all, unless you let it. So why protect it with your life.

But relationships on the other hand pose a massive threat to all.

The other person within these situations has the means to destroy a person's mental health in a few swift blows, if they have the know - how.

So why be so flippant in the approach to relationships, in that I mean just meeting someone on the street is risky.

I HAVE THINGS TO SAY

I hate not knowing.
If I ask it's not to stress or harm anyone in any way.
If I do ask it is important to me and is not something to be pushed aside.
I can and will put up with a lot but there does come a point.
Trust is paramount in most cases, once gone very hard to retrieve.
I hate think things which hurt as most people, especially if it can be avoided by a simple conversation.
I try and live by what I say and do.

Tell them they want to know

Well the end product is death, whether it's in mind, spirit or body, it is the outcome.

Maybe I'm paranoid but things wrong or right, can be seen in this way.

One could think when people meet on any level, whether as partner or friends or even just on street for first time, there is an element of what can this person do for me. It's possible that it's a natural thing which is built in to humans or because of the dog eat dog concept where there is survival of the fittest, or due to the way society has made it.

The question I pose to myself is how far would one go to get whatever it is that person has that you want.

I speak of myself because I am the only person I know, I may speculate on others but take them as non fact.

I find myself sometimes asking for something without asking.

In that I mean I could be in situation where I know that someone has something, whether it be money, a tool, the means to get somewhere or just information that I would like to have. I would lead the conversation into a topic where the item can be mentioned. With that, depending on the person, normally that item is offered to me.

This is not intentional. And I do think that I have to refuse it because, the same situation has happened with me on the receiving end. The word sucker comes to mind.

Sometimes it is not as easy as that, and gentle persuasion is used. Like keep mentioning the item or think by not talking.

That is a simple example.

But on the other hand it is possible to gain the upper hand if you're the person with the item.

If realized that what you have is important to the other person, doing the right thing or wrong thing depending how you see it can gain you control to a certain extent of that person. This can be good if your intention is good; if not it can be fatal for that person involved. Even more so if you have no intention to give that the item at all.

With this control the sky the limit, in what you can get that person to do. All depends on how important the item is to them. This can be seen to be used by person from years 0 to death.

In both these examples it is possible to do enormous amount of good, but also can cause a hell of a lot of damage.

This I see as a way of life for most people of today, old and young.

Few days in solitary

Although I have not been here, this title is just a feeling... I could call this the beginning of the end, but it would not be timed right as the beginning started without me knowing....

Taking most of my writing into consideration, a few days inside closed doors, with only thoughts and stimulants from outside curtained windows and prompts which I mentioned before. You can't help and I mean can't help but enter into whatever is put into or in front of you...

A reality with feeling... vision... substance. Which you cannot deny but only question...

I have said once that believing is seeing, not seeing is believing... A few days in this situation can confirm this, not only seeing but feeling and living...

Also within this time, build up of feelings of frustration, which breeds anger, reasoning and clarity, causes moments of unexplained vents of energy which make perfect sense within the fame of mind that the situation creates? But to the reality of most world, be sectionable I think... But that's only due to what is known as the norm...

Mysteries of the mind, don't underestimate them. You'd be a fool to!

Life eh what can I say

As they say one man's pleasure is another man's pain.

Thinking about situations that seem to arise over and over again in my life and I can only put it down to a theory I state in "Tell them what they want to know"

This is that when one sees that they have the upper hand in a situation, he or she will abuse their power, and really push the boundaries of the underdog, even if the power happy one doesn't want to.

It's a case of every action has a reaction. If one says or does something to another there are only a few things that the receiver can do. If the reaction is negative then the response to that is negative, and so on and so on. So if one has a bad impression of the other in any way then a simple conversation can turn into a battle.

Free fall

Not sure what is happening to me at moment seems strange and in some ways unsettling but yet if I don't question, is calm.

Just thinking about life and how it seem to guide you through things without you realizing it, but if you can look back and think about what has happened in the last hour, day, week before you can see the logic in what has just occurred,

But, and there is always a but. This happening has no thought for you, despite your feeling, your wants or needs. It's just carries on going sometimes leaving you an in state, sometimes in good spirits, but it just keeps going.

The ability to forget is an asset to this process, but at the same time is a downfall.

In the positive to forget, you can have had something and then it's gone, you don't miss it because you don't remember it.

In the negative if you don't remember it, you don't know when it happens again. And if it does happen again you don't know whether is good or bad.

Me, I know what I have had and I know when it is no longer there.

At the same time if it was significant I will miss it. And whether I can do something about it or not, will feel like something is missing. In this I mean I have a feeling that something is just not right. In life I can't get away from this.

Well if you can't change it, live with it. Not that we have much choice. Or do we?

JUST HAD A THOUGHT!

It could be that Im trying to defy the natural process of my mind.

This could be why I have so much conflict within myself.

But if I think something, which to my knowledge is best for those concerned, the process of this conclusion will differ, and cause conflict within me. I may get into a state, and those around me will just get on with it anyway without my input. You may say why don't I just go with it. The answer is whatever I do, I get the unpleasant end of the situation. There must be a conclusion to this, which is not as unpleasing.

Going with the process will not only make me into a social outcast, but will make everyone around's life a misery.

This process of this conclusion as far as I can see is look after number one and it is ruthless in doing so. Without an anchor to ground you, one can become a nomad.

We talk about baggage, if we take all of it into account and act on it without question. We become what we know not what we think. Looks like that's the way of the world.

Conclusion to Tell them what they want to know

I think the key is in self-worth and self-belief.
In respect to fighting battles, what does it matter whether to leave a situation with the other person thinking they have won. Its what you think that matters. You have to live with you, they don't. So as long as you're reasoning is satisfying to your mind, then you win.
Armed with this you can face any situation. You don't have to exclude myself.
Due to the fact that you don't fight to the death in every situation you maintain a strong spirit. And is controlled by you and your mind, not influences and inputs.

But you have to be careful in what you believe in within yourself.

QUESTION

With all that I say, think and do. I do get to a point where it is calm collected thought which amazes me. Clear focused thought, which brings all the haphazard, manic thoughts into play to bring bliss.
This normally takes a conversation or situation with like mind people who are few and far between.
I have had a handful of moments in which this has happened without the aid of drink, drugs or any other mind altering substances. But I have achieved it on my own only a few times in the 15 years of experiencing thought processes which are branded not the norm.
But in saying that, it is not long before I will start trying to think in the manic way, which has caused pain, so much heart ache, distress me.
I guess is it that I am so familiar with the hectic thought pattern that I think I can't survive without it.
Like most things you don't know what you have until you lose it.
This confuses me because of the damage it has done over a time to me and many of the people around me. I should not yearn for this to continue.
So why do I.

Sayings

Life is not what it seems.
Believe in yourself and anything is possible.

Time is just time, but your world has a way of making things happen.

When time is an issue, then there is no life....

As I walk with the shadow of death I will fear no evil...

Perfection is a designation not a state....

The closest thing to perfection is something of constant change...

All that stimulates me becomes part of me...
Then who am I..

Self without stimulate is one's self.

In connection with ending of solitary. The world can be determined by collective thought as well as majority word and action...

World 22!